BLENHEIM PALACE

FIEL PERO DESDICHADO

WOODSTOCK · OXFORDSHIRE

'THE FINEST VIEW IN ENGLAND'

The usual approach to Blenheim is through Woodstock, past Sir William Chambers' town hall, past the Bear and the church, and along a street of well-bred Georgian fronts, brass knockers and climbing roses, intermingled with unobtrusive shops; the kind of street that might be expected eventually to lead gently out again into the mild, wooded Oxfordshire countryside.

This street is different. After the last shop it turns to the left, crosses a quadrangle and dives through a triumphal arch to spring on the visitor – suddenly and all at once – a view painstakingly designed to take the breath away.

'As we passed through the entrance archway and the lovely scenery burst upon me', wrote Lady Randolph Churchill on her first visit to Blenheim, 'Randolph said with pardonable pride, "This is the finest view in England." Looking at the lake, the bridge, the miles of magnificent park studded with old oaks . . . and the huge and stately palace, I confess I felt awed. But my

American pride forbade the admission.'

From this Woodstock entrance the towers of the palace appear some way off to the left, while far away to the right the Column of Victory, topped with its statue of the 1st Duke of Marlborough, rises nobly above the trees. But what takes the eye and holds it is the great lake and its poplared island, like a becalmed frigate, with Sir John Vanbrugh's Grand Bridge and 'Capability' Brown's hanging beech-woods beyond; all apparently so effort-less and natural, all in reality so thoughtfully and laboriously contrived. It is the view that Turner painted; the same that caused George III to exclaim, 'We have nothing to equal this!'

AND HEIRESS
...NGS OF SANDRIDGE
...HERTFORD ESQ.
...HURCHILL
...LBOROUGH

THE QUEEN'S REWARD

By the time that Queen Anne came to the throne in February 1702 John Churchill, 1st Duke of Marlborough, and his wife, Sarah, were already long-accepted members of the royal circle. Sarah, particularly, was an intimate friend of the new Queen, who had come to depend on her companionship and advice. When, later in the same year, war broke out in Europe, Marlborough, a military genius, was the obvious choice as leader of the allied troops. During 1702 and 1703 Marlborough defended Holland from invasion by the French, and in 1704 began to move forward up the Rhine valley. On 13th August a decisive battle took place on the north bank of the Danube near a small village called Blindheim, or Blenheim, where the French leader, Marshall Tallard, had fixed his lines. Here Marlborough won a great allied victory over the forces of Louis XIV, thus saving Vienna from a French invasion.

In reward for his services, the grateful Queen granted to Marlborough the Royal Manor of Woodstock and signified that she would build him there, at her own expense, a house to be called Blenheim.

DUCHESS AND ARCHITECT

The architect chosen to complete this task was John Vanbrugh, who had already proved his ability by his masterly designs for Greenwich Hospital and Castle Howard.

The Duchess of Marlborough preferred Wren to Vanbrugh and made this clear by commissioning him to build Marlborough House in St James's (1709-11) on condition that 'hee would make the contracts reasonable . . . and that hee must make my hous

Above: **Sir John Vanbrugh, the architect of Blenheim, painted by Sir Godfrey Kneller in 1710**
Left: **Sarah 1st Duchess of Marlborough wearing a mantilla, thought to be in mourning for her baby son, Charles. Painting by Sir Godfrey Kneller**

strong plain and convenient and that hee must give me his word that this building should not have the least resemblance of any thing in that called Blenheim which I had never liked but could not prevail against Sr John'. For a time the aged Sir Christopher and his son gave satisfaction, but towards the end the Duchess suspected that in the matter of building-rates 'the poor old man was being imposed upon'; and so, taking the building out of Wren's hands, she finished it as her own self-appointed surveyor and clerk of the works. It cost £50,000.

But who appointed Vanbrugh to design Blenheim Palace? Queen Anne, said the Duchess. Vanbrugh, on the contrary, insisted that the Duke of Marlborough himself, meeting him at the playhouse, had declared his intention of building a house at

Woodstock and had asked him to design one. And to support this, Vanbrugh produced a warrant, dated 9th June 1705 and signed by Lord Godolphin, the Treasurer, appointing him 'at the request and desire of the Duke' surveyor (i.e. architect) for Blenheim, which 'His Grace had resolv'd to build'. Nowhere in the warrant or in any subsequent warrant or contract was there one word of Queen or Crown.

Was this important? Immensely; because when Queen Anne replaced the Duchess, in her role as Keeper of the Privy Purse, by Mrs Abigail Masham, Treasury payments for the building of Blenheim dwindled and ceased. Masons and others who had not been paid for years quite naturally sued the Duke who, just as understandably, resented and resisted the idea of having to pay for his own reward.

BLENHEIM'S STORY
THE INSCRIPTION ON THE EAST GATE

The inscription on the East Gate declares that:

> Under the auspices of a munificent sovereign this house was built for John Duke of Marlborough, and his Duchess Sarah, by Sir J. Vanbrugh between the years 1705 and 1722. And this Royal Manor of Woodstock, together with a grant of £240,000, towards the building of Blenheim was given by Her Majesty Queen Anne and confirmed by Act of Parliament . . .

UNDER THE AUSPICES OF A MUNIFICENT SOVEREIGN THIS HOUSE WAS BUILT FOR JOHN DUKE OF MARLBOROUGH, AND HIS DUCHESS SARAH, BY SIR J. VANBRUGH BETWEEN THE YEARS 1705 AND 1722. AND THIS ROYAL MANOR OF WOODSTOCK, TOGETHER WITH A GRANT OF £240,000, TOWARDS THE BUILDING OF BLENHEIM WAS GIVEN BY HER MAJESTY QUEEN ANNE AND CONFIRMED BY ACT OF PARLIAMENT (3. & 4. ANNE C. 4.) TO THE SAID JOHN DUKE OF MARLBOROUGH AND TO ALL HIS ISSUE MALE AND FEMALE LINEALLY DESCENDING.

But that is only a small part of the story. At least £60,000 was contributed by Marlborough and his widow towards the initial cost of the building; and of course a great many thousands have been spent on it since.

Queen Anne's generosity was regal indeed, but if only she had made it clear at the outset how much she meant to give! At the time the present was given, so high was Marlborough's favour, so close the friendship between Queen and Duchess, that any hint of a limit to the royal bounty – much less anything so formal and cold as a written agreement – would have been unthinkable. Later there were plenty found to cast doubt on the Queen's intentions and even to deny that she had given such a present at all.

As victory followed victory (Ramillies, 1706; Oudenarde, 1708; Malplaquet, 1709) no one, except those few who were plotting it, dreamed of Marlborough's fall from favour. He said himself that he never would have believed it possible that so staunch a friendship could so soon have been lost. Perhaps if duty had not kept him overseas, the patience and diplomacy which had worked marvels for his country might also have preserved peace, if not love, between 'Mrs Freeman' (his Duchess) and 'Mrs Morley' (the Queen). As it was, he could not be there to check Sarah from 'teasing and tormenting' her royal mistress in such a way as to make it so much the easier for the soft-spoken Mrs Masham, supported by Robert Harley, Earl of Oxford, to supplant her.

In the spring of 1710 the Duchess had her last and most distressing interview with the Queen; and in the summer of 1712 all building at Blenheim ceased. The amount then owing to masons, carvers and others (including Vanbrugh) was £45,000, though no less than £220,000 had already been paid out.

From 1712 to 1714 the Marlboroughs were abroad in what the Duchess called 'a sort of exile'. They returned the day after Queen Anne died 'My lord Duke,' said George I to Marlborough, 'I hope your troubles are now all over.' A knighthood was conferred on Vanbrugh, and after the Queen's 'debts' had been looked into and the Blenheim debt acknowledged, the Duke decided to finish the palace at his own expense, with Vanbrugh as architect, and Nicholas Hawksmoor assisting him, as before.

But there were difficulties. Men of skill and standing, like Grinling Gibbons and the Edward Strongs (who part-owned the famous quarries at Taynton, near Burford, and had worked as chief masons on St Paul's), had been paid by the Treasury only a third of what was due to them for Blenheim. That was bad enough. But now they were told that the rates they had been charging were Crown rates. For the Duke they must lower them. This, for reputation's sake and for other good reasons, they could not bring themselves to do. That is why Gibbons completed only one of the four marble doorcases in the Saloon and why foreman-masons took over in 1716, and carried on at the lower rates their masters could not afford to accept.

The summer of 1716, then, saw a resumption of work at Blenheim, but by November Vanbrugh had left in a rage, never to return as surveyor or architect. Differences with the Duchess about costs had been brought to a head by her violent criticisms which, coupled with her ill-usage of him in other matters, made it, as he told her, impracticable to continue.

'You have your end, Madam,' he concluded, 'for I will never trouble you more unless the Duke of Marlborough recovers [from a stroke] so far [as] to shelter me from such intolerable Treatment.

'I shall in the meantime have only this Concern on his account (for whom I shall ever retain the greatest Veneration), that your Grace having like the Queen thought fit to get rid of a faithful servant, the Tory's will have the pleasure to See your Glassmaker, Moor, make just such an end of the Dukes Building as her Minister Harley did of his Victories for which it was erected.'

Strange guesses have been made as to the identity of the glassmaker,

n Duke of Marlborough

Moor. He was in fact James Moore, the cabinet-maker, a designer of considerable originality, referred to by the Duchess as her 'oracle; of very good sense . . . very honest and understanding in many Trades besides his own'. At Blenheim he not only made pier-glasses, a great many of which were needed, some – the Duke's idea – to reflect the pictures, but in November 1716 Moore took over from Vanbrugh and Hawksmoor as clerk of the works and factotum, assisted by one Desborough of Woodstock. It was not till after the Duke's death that Hawksmoor was recalled for the Triumphal Arch and other outworks; while Vanbrugh was in permanent and irretrievable disgrace. In 1725, when Sir John and Lady Vanbrugh, accompanied by the Earl of Carlisle and party, presented themselves at

John 1st Duke of Marlborough, the national hero for whom Blenheim was built, by Closterman

Hawksmoor's two-year-old arch, they were refused admittance even to the park. Vanbrugh did at least see the arch; and had managed to snatch a glimpse of the palace itself six years previously, while the Duchess was away. He died in 1726.

THE EAST GATE

If the inscription on the East Gate may be said to give the main theme of the Blenheim story, then its structure strikes the keynote of the palace itself. 'I thought it absolutely best', wrote Vanbrugh of another of his buildings (Kimbolton), 'to give it something of the castle air.' Blenheim too was a castle and was known as such in his day. Vanbrugh looked upon it, as he admitted, 'much more as an intended Monument of the Queen's glory than a private Habitation for the Duke of Marlborough', though it was of course celebrating military glory, in which Marlborough had had a giant's share. Blenheim, then, had to be castle, citadel, monument and – less important – private house. Its main entries must speak of strength triumphant; and undoubtedly this East Gate, as Vanbrugh left it, spoke bluntly of that.

But there was yet another and purely practical reason for the gate's massiveness: it was to carry the great cistern upon which the more important

The Duke of Marlborough's standard flies from the East Gate when he is in residence. The inscription (see page 8) **was added by the 9th Duke**

half of the palace, containing the private apartments and kitchen, would depend for water-supply.

Grinling Gibbons, famed chiefly for wood carving, was responsible for the stone urns, which he carved in 1708 for £7 apiece. The two statues are also thought to be from his workshop; sole survivors of the eighteen graces and virtues he contracted to set up on the quadrants flanking the north portico. The lion heads, wreaths and laurels were all added by Sir William Chambers (architect of Somerset House) in 1773. The gates, bearing the Marlborough arms, weigh 17 tons. Made by Bramah, they were shown at the Great Exhibition of 1851.

It is from this gate (Flagstaff Lodge, as it is sometimes called) that the flag is flown when the Duke is in residence.

THE EAST COURT
The Base or Kitchen Court

Here are the 'Cover'd Ways for Servants', which, in their 'extravagance', shocked the 1st Duchess. She insisted too on less costly stone. The material for this court was to have been Headington stone, cheap but not of first quality, till Vanbrugh thought of the stone quarried at Heythrop, 'still cheaper and better'. However, it has recently been restored. The most dependable stones of all came from Taynton, Barrington and Cornbury (in Wychwood Forest) and these were used for the more important parts of the palace, according to colour and weather resistance.

The orangery in the south-east corner of this court was, in the 4th Duke's time, a theatre, 'fitted up in a style of peculiar elegance' in grey, blue and white. It seated two hundred and was last used as a theatre in 1789. The stage end has since been divided off as a muniment room. Next to this, on the west, are offices, including the Estate Office and the Audit Room, which was originally the kitchen.

Vanbrugh's vast kitchen, rib-vaulted by Henry Banks, who built the East Gate and the colonnades of the Great Court, is in the south-west corner of the East Court. Long since disused as a kitchen, it has been criticised for its remoteness from the dining-rooms, in the heart of the main building. But in Anne's day etiquette and 'state' were infinitely more important than hot food; and to tolerate the smell of cooking, in state or private apartments, was out of the question. The laundry, correspondingly huge, looked onto this court; and the 30-foot (9-metre) walls of the adjoining drying-ground were designed to transform a light breeze into something approaching a whirlwind.

The clock (1710) is by Langley Bradley, who also made the original 'Turritt' clock in St Paul's Cathedral. The dial seen from the East Court is level with the movement (restored by Vulliamy, another eminent maker). The other three dials are on a higher storey so as to be visible from the park. Bradley's bill, including the three bells, came to £303 16s. 3d., but was reduced by £100. The tower, during building, was called Townsend's Tower, after its mason, John Townsend of Oxford. Sarah referred to it as 'a great thing where the Clock is and which is Called a Tower of great Ornament'. It cost £1,435 19s. 7d.

THE GREAT COURT
OR NORTH FORECOURT

The archway beneath Townsend's clock tower leads to the Great Court, the dramatic prelude to the main front of the palace. But remember to look back at the coroneted dial and see the two grotesque lions savaging the protesting cocks of France. These are among the best stonework of Grinling Gibbons, who was responsible at Blenheim for enrichments in stone and marble to the tune of just over £4,000. In this Great Court, as well as the lions (£25 each), there are his trophies on the colonnades (£40 each), and his Marlborough coat of arms (£75) in the tympanum of the portico. Gibbons' workshop was in the stables block

(the only part of the west court completed) and out of it came all the urns, vases and finials and most of the statues. For Pallas on the north pediment he charged £28, and for each of the chained captives above her he charged the same.

Much has had to be renewed here, mainly in the form of finials and statues; and to Charles 9th Duke of Marlborough, we owe the most ambitious restoration of all. With his French architect, Achille Duchêne, he worked to restore the setting of Blenheim as far as possible in accordance with Vanbrugh's original design. To some extent he was bound to compromise. He made no attempt to re-establish the Great Parterre on the south side, but he laid out two delightful formal gardens, on the east and on the west. He did not, after much consideration, carry out Vanbrugh's conception of a monolithic gate and colonnade to enclose the Great Court, but he did skilfully undo 'Capability'

Brown's abuse of this same forecourt and entirely repaved it (1900–10). Another of his achievements was the replanting of the Great Avenue of elms, which stretched 3,000 yards (2,700 metres) from the Column of Victory to the Ditchley Gate, and was said, albeit

Stone sculpture by Grinling Gibbons: (*above*) **the British lion savaging the cock of France, on the clock tower, and** (*below*) **a trophy set on the chapel colonnade**

The Great Court and north front; reproduced from an early eighteenth-century engraving

on slight authority, to represent the lines of the opposing armies as they stood arrayed at the Battle of Blenheim.

Blenheim had first to be a monument to the Queen's glory. This had to be achieved within the limits of contemporary conventions which insisted on symmetry, formality and a disposition of state rooms – ante-room, drawing-room, bedroom – from which there could be no deviation. For any architect, let alone one of short experience, the task was all but superhuman; and yet it is hard if not impossible to imagine any other architect, of any age, accomplishing that task so well.

It is not only the size of the buildings and courts (covering 7 acres/2.8 hectares) which makes it impossible to see and judge Blenheim at a glance. Vanbrugh planned, as Wren always insisted, 'in perspective'. As a result the building is 'good' from almost all points of the compass and from varying distances, though perhaps least so head-on to its main fronts and at close quarters to them. Blenheim can be exciting to look at in all seasons and at all hours; never more so than by moonlight or by floodlight. Here on the north front it surges to its crescendo. It is the supreme example of the style of architecture known as English Baroque.

THE ROOFS

The roofs of Blenheim are like a small town on another planet. The records

show that the choosing of the ornaments, to please both Duchess and architect, was a most laborious business in which countless models were hoisted. Some are glorified chimneys – unromantic essentials which Vanbrugh, unlike some of his successors, knew how to school into an eloquent skyline. Most striking of all perhaps are the 30-foot (9-metre) finials rising from the square towers. For these too Grinling Gibbons contracted: 'the Scrolls a flower De Luce [fleur-de-lys] revers'd and Corronett upon the Same'.

THE STONE

When the masons at Blenheim were at their busiest, an army of men and horses brought the stone from more than twenty quarries. The tracks to some of these quarries turned after rain to mire. In 1710, when the carters demanded an extra penny a foot to fetch large blocks of fine stone from Barrington, the Duchess's refusal delayed progress on the main part of the building: the very thing she most wished to avoid. Lichened monoliths of Cornbury stone, poised above a lake in the heart of Wychwood Forest and

intended perhaps for the unfinished stables court, still await the Blenheim wagons. For the steps to the north and south porticoes, Vanbrugh prescribed Plymouth Moor stone, and since this was long in coming, the Duchess found herself, as late as 1716, without any worthy means of entry. By that time she was fully prepared to attribute such shortcomings to malice. For a number of reasons, however, she found it impossible to live in the palace before 1719, and when she did, she complained that the stone aggravated her gout.

THE GREAT HALL

The Great Hall is chiefly remarkable for its proportions (it is 67 feet, or 20 metres, high), for its Thornhill ceiling, and for its stone enrichments 'Cutt Extrordingry rich and sunk very deep' by Gibbons and his assistants, who also carved the arms of Queen Anne on the keystone of the main arch, which spans a minstrels' gallery, originally open to the Saloon beyond.

The bust of Marlborough, over the Saloon door, has an inscription in Latin and in English. Sarah particularly liked the last line:

'Nor cou'd Augustus better calm mankind'

which she knew 'to bee an exact description of the Dear Duke of Marlboroughs temper'.

The hall ceiling, painted in 1716 by Sir James Thornhill, shows Marlborough victorious, with the battle order at Blenheim spread for view. Thornhill was also to have painted the Saloon and the Long Library, but the Duchess suspected him of sharp practice in charging (for the hall) twenty-five shillings (£1.25) a yard for the murals in *grisaille* – 'not', she considered, 'worth half-a-crown [12.5p] a yard' – as well as for the 'historical part' (ceiling) in colour; and so, in spite of his spirited and carefully finished drafts for the Saloon, she changed her mind and commissioned a French artist, Louis Laguerre: a reversal of what had happened at St Paul's, where Laguerre had lost the dome decoration to Thornhill. The ceiling panels of the Long Library remained undecorated.

The long, vaulted corridors running to the wings from the north and south sides of the Great Hall are typical of Vanbrugh, as is the staircase, concealed by the arcaded eastern wall. (There was originally intended to be another staircase behind the western wall.) Good, simple ironwork supports the handrail and screens the balcony. None, directed the Duchess, was to be bespoke till she had seen the pattern.

One exciting idea, sketched by Thornhill but never adopted, was to treat the hall as a vast guard-room, its walls glinting with suits of armour and with great wheels of silver suns made of pistols and cutlasses, as in the guard-rooms at Windsor and Hampton Court.

The complicated lock for the hall doors was copied from a lock found on the gates of Warsaw. With it goes a huge coroneted key.

The bronze bust of the 9th Duke of Marlborough is by Epstein. In the corridor leading from the Great Hall to the Long Library two white marble busts by the American sculptor Waldo Story are of the 9th Duke and his Duchess Consuelo.

The elaborate lock in brass on the doors of the main entrance, copied from a lock on the gates of Warsaw

Left: **The Great Hall ceiling, painted by Sir James Thornhill in 1716: Marlborough kneels to Britannia and proffers a plan of the Battle of Blenheim**

The arms of Queen Anne, carved by Grinling Gibbons, key the arch leading to the Saloon

Bust of the 9th Duke of Marlborough by Sir Jacob Epstein

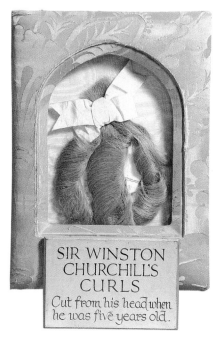

SIR WINSTON CHURCHILL'S CURLS
Cut from his head when he was five years old.

SIR WINSTON CHURCHILL

West of the Great Hall lies the suite of apartments once allotted to Marlborough's domestic chaplain, Dean Jones, whose caricature Laguerre painted in the Saloon. In one of these rooms, on 30th November 1874, Sir Winston Churchill was born. 'At Blenheim', he declared, 'I took two very important decisions: to be born and to marry [for he proposed in the Temple of Diana]. I am happily content with the decisions I took on both those occasions.'

When Sir Winston was asked whether, just before his birth, his mother, Lady Randolph, was attending a ball in the Long Library or was out with a shooting-party in the park, he replied, 'Although present on that occasion, I have no clear recollection of the events leading up to it.'

'We can look back now on the pattern of Sir Winston's life', wrote the late Duke of Marlborough, 'and see or think we see a pleasing inevitability. His birth at Blenheim, his proposal of marriage here beside the lake, his burial at Bladon – these things form a mosaic which seems almost too neat to be true. Yet it was only by chance that he happened to be born in the house built for the man – John 1st Duke of Marlborough – whom he so much admired.

'Sir Winston had a strong sense of family. If he did not worship his ancestors he came near it in his protagonism of Marlborough and of his own father, Lord Randolph Churchill. His affection was strong for his family and for his friends, of whom my father was one. When I was a boy he visited us often at Blenheim. My father also invited Sir Winston's brother and Lord Birkenhead and they livened things up with wild games of "French and English" in the hall.

'Beyond question Blenheim made for Sir Winston the ideal

The birth room of Sir Winston Churchill

background, and I don't mean only for his paintings. At times, for example when he was researching for his life of Marlborough, it must have given him inspiration; but although, before I was born, he was heir to the dukedom, I doubt if he hankered much for the place itself. Much as he cared for Blenheim, it would not have appealed to him to go down in history as its owner. He had other and better ideas.' (*Weekend Telegraph*, 9th September 1966)

Vanbrugh's north-south line of axis for Blenheim passes through the Column of Victory, the Great Hall, the Saloon and the tower of Bladon

Above: **Sir Winston Churchill's painting of the Great Hall**

Left: **Sir Winston Churchill at Blenheim in 1958**

pilgrimage for ever. The remains of his dearly loved wife, Clementine, Baroness Spencer-Churchill, DBE, who died on 12th December 1977, now lie there peacefully beside him, as they would both have wished.

In the Churchill Exhibition, near the birth room, can be seen Oscar Nemon's bronze of Sir Winston and Lady Churchill, and Sir Winston's painting of the Great Hall at Blenheim. Before he had finished that painting, the 10th Duchess expressed her admiration. 'Do you like it, Mary?' he said, 'Then you shall have it for Blenheim.' The exhibits vary from Churchill's lively letters to a piece of shrapnel which, in the 1914-18 war, fell between himself and his cousin, the 9th Duke of Marlborough and, as the inscription testifies, might easily have ended their lifelong friendship.

Church, which may be seen from the Saloon and beside which tower Sir Winston is buried. Thus physically and symbolically are linked the places of his birth and burial.

By choosing to be buried beside his parents in a village churchyard, Sir Winston made Bladon a place of

Right: **The grave at Bladon**

On the right of the wide corridor as you leave Sir Winston's birth room hangs Closterman's large painting of the 1st Duke and Duchess of Marlborough, their four daughters (Henrietta, Anne, Elizabeth and Mary) and their son, the 1st Marquis of Blandford, who died of smallpox at the age of seventeen. After Marlborough's death in 1722, his eldest daughter, Henrietta, became Duchess in her own right; and when she died in 1733, the dukedom passed to Charles, son of Anne, Countess of Sunderland (wearing red in this picture); while his younger brother, John, was to be the ancestor of the Earls Spencer.

In the China Cabinets, outside the Green Drawing-room, are displays of Meissen (Dresden) and Sèvres porcelain. The Meissen, with sliced-lemon handles to the tureens, was presented to the 3rd Duke by the King of Poland in exchange for a pack of staghounds.

Below: **A Meissen tureen, part of a large service presented to the 3rd Duke by the King of Poland in exchange for a pack of staghounds**

Above: **The 1st Duke and Duchess of Marlborough with their family, painted in 1693 by Closterman**

Above: **Sarah 1st Duchess of Marlborough at cards with Lady Fitzharding, by Sir Godfrey Kneller**

Right: **Caroline 4th Duchess of Marlborough dancing her baby on her knee, by Sir Joshua Reynolds**

Below: **A clock by Gosselin, mounted upon a black bull**

THE GREEN DRAWING-ROOM

The Green Drawing-room and the two rooms beyond it all have their original ceilings, which were designed by Nicholas Hawksmoor, Vanbrugh's collaborator. The portraits include two famous Knellers: the Mantilla portrait of Sarah Duchess of Marlborough and, over a door, Sarah again with another of Queen Anne's ladies-in-waiting, Lady Fitzharding, at cards. The Romney over the chimney-piece is of the 4th Duke, while the Reynolds on the north wall shows his Duchess Caroline dancing her babe. On the west wall a delightful painting by Michael Wright shows Winston and Arabella, brother and sister of the 1st Duke of Marlborough. The elaborate pier-glass between the windows was made for the 4th Duke by William Ince and John Mayhew. The equally elaborate clock, mounted upon a black bull, is by Gosselin of Paris.

George Spencer, 4th Duke of Marlborough, KG, LLD, FRS, was a lifelong friend of King George III. At Blenheim, where he succeeded to the dukedom in 1758, he was extremely active, with the help of 'Capability' Brown, in improving the grounds and waters on a princely scale. His architects, Sir William Chambers and John Yenn, added the Temple of Diana and the New Bridge near Bladon. Towards the end of his life the 4th Duke became a recluse and declined to receive Lord Nelson and the Hamiltons when they called in 1802. He died in 1817.

Right: **The Green Drawing-room; over the chimney-piece is Romney's portrait of the 4th Duke**

THE RED DRAWING-ROOM

In this room, for deliberate contrast, two very large paintings face one another. The great Reynolds, dated 1778, is of the 4th Duke of Marlborough and his family. In his left hand the Duke holds a sardonyx, while his heir, the Marquis of Blandford, carries one of the cases containing the Marlborough gems. The whole family took part in private theatricals, performed in a sumptuous theatre in the orangery. The story goes that while he was painting this group at Blenheim, Sir Joshua scattered snuff; whereupon the Duchess, anxious for her carpet, sent for a footman to sweep it up. 'Go away,' said Reynolds, 'the dust you make will do more harm to my picture than my snuff to the carpet.' It is said too that he was determined to catch Lady Anne's look of fear (she was four) when she first saw him and cried out: 'I won't be painted!' Hence the mask-charade.

In the Sargent facing it the late Duke stands between his father, Charles 9th Duke, who like the 4th Duke wears Garter robes, and his mother, Consuelo (née Vanderbilt, and later to become Madame Balsan). 'Sargent', the Duchess afterwards recalled, 'chose a black dress whose wide sleeves were lined with deep rose

satin; the model had been used by Van Dyck in a portrait in the Blenheim collection.' The Vandyck referred to – of Lady Killigrew and 'the Countess of Morton' – still hangs in this room on the north wall. The chimney-piece, designed by Sir William Chambers and executed by Joseph Wilton, has a central plaque sculptured to represent the marriage of Cupid and Psyche, in imitation of the most celebrated of the Marlborough gems; while above it hangs Van Dyck's portrait of his wife. The large bronzes of Fame and Mercury are by Coysevox (1640-1720). The bronze figure on the mantelshelf is by Soldani. The mahogany doors were designed by Sir William Chambers.

Above left: **The 4th Duke and Duchess of Marlborough and their family, by Sir Joshua Reynolds**

Above: **Lady Killigrew and 'the Countess of Morton' by Van Dyck**

Below: **Mercury by Coysevox**

THE GREEN WRITING-ROOM

On the right of the chimney-piece is the well-known portrait of Marlborough, by Closterman, before which the Duke, in old age, is said to have murmured, 'This was once a man.'

On the far side of the room hangs the most famous of all the tapestries, that showing Marlborough in his hour of triumph as he accepts Marshall Tallard's surrender at the Battle of Blenheim (1704). Tallard was bundled into Marlborough's coach with two other captured generals and sent to England, to be kept prisoner at Nottingham. There he was handsomely treated; far more handsomely, in fact, than was Marlborough, whom Queen Anne, after all his victories, dismissed in 1711. As for the tapestry itself, it looks, as Sarah described it in 1740, 'as fresh as new', and the more you look into it, the more you see. For example, behind the grenadier with the captured French standard are burning water mills and a field dressing-station; behind them the village of Blindheim (Blenheim) packed with French troops; and beyond that, in the far distance, the Danube, into which the allies are driving thousands of the enemy. The tapestry on the opposite wall shows an incident at Wynendael (1708), when it was found necessary with the help of a halberd to keep the hired driver of a 'Marlbrouk' cart at his post. The portrait over the chimney-piece is of Elizabeth 3rd Duchess of Marlborough. The ceiling was designed by Vanbrugh's partner, Nicholas Hawksmoor.

Above: **Sir Winston Churchill, father of the 1st Duke of Marlborough**

Below: **The Battle of Blenheim tapestry; the detail below shows Blindheim (Blenheim) packed with French troops and, in the centre, burning water mills and a casualty station**

Above: **The Saloon ceiling painted by Laguerre**
Right: **Frescoes in the Saloon by Laguerre, doorcases by Grinling Gibbons**

Below: **Silver centrepiece of Marlborough, still on horseback after his victory at Blenheim, writing his famous dispatch to his Duchess**

THE SALOON

This is the state dining-room, now used by the family once a year, on Christmas Day. The table is laid with a Minton service and with silver gilt. The silver centrepiece, standing on a separate table, shows Marlborough, still on horseback after his victory at the Battle of Blenheim, writing the famous dispatch, now displayed in the next state room. The murals and painted ceiling are the work of Louis Laguerre (1663–1721). His charge was £500. Among the people he chose to caricature can be seen (above his signature) himself, neighboured by Dean Jones, Marlborough's chaplain, whom the Duchess disliked but tolerated because he could make the Duke laugh and would take a hand at cards. The marble doorcases were undertaken by Grinling Gibbons, but only one of them had been set up when in 1712 a halt was called. Though work was resumed in 1716, Gibbons never returned. He died in 1721. The overdoors are emblazoned with the two-headed eagle crest of the Duke of Marlborough as a Prince of the Holy Roman Empire.

From the Saloon portico can be seen the site of the Great Parterre and beyond it the tower of Bladon Church, where Sir Winston Churchill, his wife and his parents are buried. It was from this portico that Sir Winston addressed a vast audience at a Conservative rally in August 1947.

Above: **The First State Room;
the gilded overdoor is typical of
the 9th Duke's redecoration**

Right: **First State Room; over
the chimney-piece is Duran's
portrait of the 9th Duchess. In
the left foreground is
Marlborough's
dispatch from the battle-
field of Blenheim**

Left: **An Italian cradle
given to the 9th Duchess
by her mother**

THREE STATE ROOMS

The three apartments intercom-
municating between the Saloon and the
Long Library, on the south front, are
known as the First, Second and Third
State Rooms. The third is sometimes
called the Boule Room, after the
furniture it contains. The walls of all
three rooms are hung with tapestries of
Marlborough's campaigns.
Marlborough himself in fact
commissioned them of the designer,

de Hondt, and the Brussels weaver, Judocus de Vos. 'It is the realistic fidelity in every detail,' wrote Dr Reid, 'no less than the artistic beauty of these tapestries which commands admiration; and the circumstance that they are almost contemporary immeasurably enhances their appeal.'

THE FIRST STATE ROOM

The tapestry on the right-hand wall of the First State Room, next to the Saloon, shows Marlborough approaching the Schellenberg, a fiercely defended hilltop fortress taken by the allies on their way to Blenheim. In the foreground, dragoons are loading their horses with fascines, or faggots, to help the infantry cross the enemy's trenches; while in the background the walled city of Donauworth prepares its defences. The other tapestries in this room are of the siege of Lille, the lines of Brabant and the Battle of Malplaquet (1709).

Over the chimney-piece Carolus Duran's portrait of Consuelo 9th Duchess of Marlborough, at the age of seventeen, catches the eye. 'My mother', she remembered, 'wished my portrait to bear comparison with those of preceding duchesses who had been painted by Gainsborough, Reynolds, Romney and Lawrence. In that proud and lovely line I still stand over the mantelpiece of one of the state rooms, with a slightly disdainful and remote look as if very far away in thought.'

In this state room too are the cradle in which she rocked the 10th Duke; the 1st Duke's hastily scribbled dispatch from the battlefield of Blenheim, to tell Duchess and Queen of 'a glorious victory'; and the Blenheim Standard, sent as quit-rent to the Sovereign at Windsor each year since the Battle of Blenheim on the anniversary date (13th August). The chairs, by Hertaut, are from Versailles.

The *boiseries*, or gilded woodwork, in these state rooms were commissioned by the 9th Duke soon after his accession in 1892, at a time when, as he afterwards admitted, he was 'young and uninformed'. The French decoration, he added, was quite out of scale. In the opinion of present-day experts, however, the Duke was too modest. The craftsmanship of his team of cabinet-makers, imported from Paris, was superb; highly skilled as they were in copying the *boiseries* of Louis XIV's bedroom at Versailles.

Quit-rent standard presented to the Sovereign as 'rent' for Blenheim on every anniversary of the Battle of Blenheim (13th August)

The Schellenberg tapestry: Marlborough prepares to storm the fortress, on his way to Blenheim

THE SECOND STATE ROOM

In the Second State Room Louis XIV himself, painted
by Mignard, hangs in the place of honour above the
chimney-piece. Yet in the tapestries flanking that portrait
we are reminded of Marlborough, who outmanoeuvred
the Sun King's troops at Bouchain (1711). The furniture
includes commodes by Migeon and a pair of blue-john
candelabra made by Matthew Boulton. The bronzes on
the console tables between the windows are particularly
fine. The baby in bronze is the 10th Duke, by Fuchs.

Above: **The Bouchain tapestry. The detail shows a dog
with what appear to be horse's hooves**

Below: **One of a pair of blue-john candelabra
by Matthew Boulton**

**Hercules and
the Centaur,
seventeenth-
century Italian
bronze**

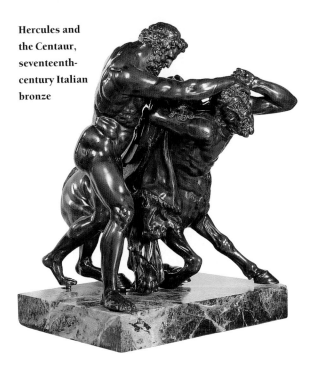

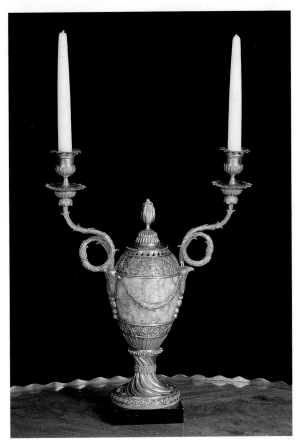

The Kakiemon vase

**The kneeling Venus
by Coysevox**

THE THIRD STATE ROOM

The Third State Room, originally a state
bedchamber, has magnificent Boule furniture, rich
tapestry and Seeman's portrait of Marlborough
studying a plan of Bouchain with Colonel
Armstrong, whom Sarah was later to call in for the
park waterworks. 'I really think that picture of your
grandfather with Mr. Armstrong', Sarah told her
granddaughter, the Duchess of Bedford, 'as like him
as ever I saw, and he [Seeman] was so humble as to
ask me 17 guineas [£17.85] for both figures.'

Above: **John 1st Duke of Marlborough with his chief engineer, Colonel Armstrong, by Seeman**
Below: **One of a pair of Boule coffers and stands**

In the middle of the mantelshelf beneath this painting stands the Kakiemon vase, a fine example of Japanese porcelain of the late seventeenth century. The large tapestry on the north wall shows Marlborough victorious again at Oudenarde (1708). He is said to have drunk from the Venetian glass goblet which stands in a glass case on the right after the Battle of Malplaquet (1709). Outstanding among the bronzes on the table (window side) is that of the kneeling Venus by Coysevox. The carpet is a Savonnerie.

THE LONG LIBRARY

This room, 180 feet (55 metres) long, was designed by Vanbrugh as a picture gallery. At one time Van Dyck's equestrian Charles I (now in the National Gallery) hung at its northern end, where the organ stands today. The organ itself originally stood in the central bay. The famous Sunderland Library, created between 1710 and 1728, was housed in this room until it was sold in 1882. The present library was largely collected by the 9th Duke.

The extraordinarily fine stucco decoration of the ceiling, including the two false domes, is by Isaac Mansfield (1725). If the 1st Duchess had not insisted on lower rates, Sir James Thornhill would most probably have painted allegorical scenes on the ceiling panels.

The full-length portraits on the east wall include those of Queen Anne, King William III and the 1st Duke of Marlborough. Portraits of three of the 1st Duke's daughters – Anne (Countess of Sunderland), Elizabeth (Countess of Bridgwater) and Mary (Duchess of Montagu) – also hang here.

Since Vanbrugh built from east to west, so that the family might live in the east wing while the rest was being finished, this western room was one of the last to be decorated, the work being done to the careful patterns Nicholas Hawksmoor had left behind. Between the lines of Hawksmoor's letters to the Duchess (1722–5) plainly runs his anxiety about the finishing of this great room. 'Ther's none can judg so well of the designe as the person who composed it,' he reminds her in 1725, 'therefore I should beg leave to take a Convenient time to Slip downe . . .' On evidence of style the marble doorcase too, erected from 1723 to 1725, may well have originated from Hawksmoor's inspired pencil; and indeed, as Laurence Whistler observes, 'though Blenheim as a whole is

Vanbrugh's, yet there is not one detail of which one could say with certainty that Hawksmoor had not designed it'.

Of the statue of Queen Anne, the Duchess told her favourite grand-daughter, in 1735, 'I am going to Rysbrack to make a bargain with him for a fine statue of Queen Anne, which I will put up in the bow window room with a proper inscription. It will be a very fine thing and though but one figure will cost me £300. I have a satisfaction in showing this respect to her, because her kindness to me was real. And what happened afterwards

was compassed by the contrivance of such as are in power now.'

She commissioned Rysbrack too for Marlborough's bust in white marble which now stands in this library's central bay. The pedestal was designed by Sir William Chambers and executed by Richard Hayward in 1772, to support an antique head of Alexander the Great, now in the Great Hall.

The Willis organ, at the north end, was installed by the 8th Duke and his American Duchess, Lilian, in 1891.

The bust of Marlborough and the statue of Queen Anne, both by John Michael Rysbrack, were commissioned by Sarah 1st Duchess of Marlborough during her widowhood of twenty-two years

To
The Memory
of
QUEEN ANN
Under Whose Auspices
JOHN DUKE of MARLBOROUGH
Conquered
And to Whose Munificence
He And His Posterity
with Gratitude
Owe the Possession
of
BLENHEIM
A·D· MDCCXXXX·VI·

Right: **The marble doorcase of
the Long Library attributed
to Nicholas Hawksmoor**

Below: **Anne Countess of
Sunderland (1684-1716),
from whom the Earls
Spencer and the Dukes of
Marlborough descend**
Below right: **Coronets of the
Duke and Duchess
of Marlborough**

When the Duke died in the following year, the moving inscription for the front of the organ was found scribbled upon a scrap of paper torn from *The Times*.

This library once housed the dispatches of John Duke of Marlborough, as well as his wife's correspondence and account of her conduct as Queen Anne's Mistress of the Robes. (They were donated to the British Library in 1974.) There are, too, Sir Winston Churchill's manuscripts for the biography of his father, Lord Randolph; and a delightful book of flower paintings by Susan 5th Duchess of Marlborough (1767-1841), when she was Lady Blandford.

Coronation robes, liveries and uniforms are displayed in the central bay with, in the foreground, the coronets of the present Duke and Duchess, and a cap worn by Queen Anne.

'This Gallery, from one part or other of it,' declared Vanbrugh in 1709, 'shows everything worth seeing about the Seat.'

Out of the Long Library windows can be seen the 9th Duke's Water Terrace Gardens, a work to which he and Duchêne devoted much thought during the nineteen-twenties. The lake seems to run on from the top terrace's edge, a feature which greatly pleased the Duke. 'It is certainly a stroke of genius on your part,' the Duke told his French architect, 'bringing the water-line up to the first terrace. I certainly should not have thought of this idea myself and I doubt any English architect would have.'

In
MEMORY
of
HAPPY DAYS
&
AS A TRIBUTE TO
THIS GLORIOUS HOME
WE LEAVE THY VOICE TO SPEAK
WITHIN THESE WALLS
IN YEARS TO COME
WHEN OURS ARE
STILL.
18   91

THE CHAPEL

On 24th May 1732, Marlborough's widow wrote
to Sir Phillip Yorke, 'The Chappel is finish'd and
more than half the Tomb there ready to set up all
in Marble Decorations of Figures, Trophies, Medals
with their inscriptions and in short everything that
could do the Duke of Marlborough Honour and
Justice. This is all upon the Wall of one side the
Chappel. The rest of it is finish'd decently,
substantially and very plain. And considering how
many Wonderful Figures and Whirligigs I have
seen Architects finish a Chappel withal, that are of
no Manner of Use but to laugh at, I must confess I
cannot help thinking that what I have designed for
this Chappel may as reasonably be call'd finishing
of it, as the Pews and Pulpit.'

The tomb, designed by Kent, was carried
out by Rysbrack for £2,200. An unsigned
memorandum records that 'The Battle upon the
Basso Relievo is to be what her Grace shall direct'.
Sarah chose for it the subject of the Blenheim
tapestry: the surrender of Marshall Tallard at the
Battle of Blenheim. The memorial is to the 1st Duke
and Duchess and their two sons: the 1st Marquis of
Blandford, who at seventeen died of smallpox, at
Cambridge; and his brother Charles, who died in
infancy. The four daughters are not mentioned.
Marlborough was buried in Westminster Abbey
and reinterred here when his Duchess died in 1744.

The large statues flanking the sarcophagus
are of History with her quill and Fame with her
trumpet; and the sarcophagus itself crushes the last
enemy of all, Envy.

Thanks to the 1st Earl of Godolphin, who
altered Vanbrugh's plan, the orientation of the
chapel is unusual, the high altar being at the west.
Much alteration also occurred during the
nineteenth century. The marble pulpit was sent to
Waddesdon Church and the font to a Woodstock
chapel, while some of the old pews survive in the
nearby church at Combe. The statue of Lord
Randolph Churchill looks down from the south
wall to church furnishings - organ, woodwork,
marble-balustraded steps - which are all Victorian.

'Mornings began with prayers in
the chapel at nine-thirty', remembered Consuelo
9th Duchess. 'At the toll of the bell housemaids
would drop their dusters, footmen their trays,
housemen their pails, carpenters their ladders,
electricians their tools, kitchenmaids their pans,
laundrymaids their linen, and all rush to reach the
chapel in time.'

**Rysbrack's
monument to
the 1st Duke
and Duchess of
Marlborough
and their two
sons, both of
whom died
young**

PARK & GARDENS

THE FORMAL GARDENS

The visitor having tea in the Arcade Rooms beneath the Long Library or on the terrace looks down to the lake across the Water Terraces. Years of thought and work were devoted to these by the 9th Duke in the nineteen-twenties. The key to their design lies in the Bernini river-gods' fountain on the second terrace. A scale-model for the famous fountain in Rome's Piazza Navona, this was given to the 1st Duke and was venerated by the 9th, who was determined to give Vanbrugh's palace the majestic, formal setting he knew it deserved. With the help of the French landscape-architect Achille Duchêne, this had already been brought about on the north front, where Brown had grassed over the forecourt, and on the east, where the Duke had created a formal garden centring on the Mermaid Fountain designed by Waldo Story. The making of the western terraces presented almost insuperable problems, but the Duke and his architect solved them, and might have gone on to remake the Great Parterre on the south, had time and money allowed.

The Great Parterre, nearly half a mile (800 metres) long and as wide as the south front which overlooked it, had been a formal garden created by Vanbrugh with the help of Queen Anne's gardener, Henry Wise, and an army of labourers. It had a 'military' framework of bastions and curtain walls, like a fortress about to be stormed and captured from Louis XIV, whose 30-ton marble bust, taken from the gates of Tournai, a Marlborough conquest, was forced to look down on it from the porticoed centrepiece above the Saloon.

The curtain walls, with eight great round bastions, each more than 100 feet (30 metres) wide, supported a terraced walk from which the stroller looked out to the park or down into the parterre itself. The garden was patterned in dwarf box, sand and crushed brick, leading to a six-sided formal wilderness, called the Woodwork, which contained shaped shrubs and clipped bushes brought from Wise's nurseries at Brompton Park. There were formal pools with fountains and, as at Kensington Palace, lime-arched walks, carpeted here with fine sand from Queen Pool. This was no flower garden. It was an architect's garden carried out in brick, in stone and in evergreen topiary.

Many thousands of flowers – iris, hyacinth, narcissus, violet, carnation, Brompton stock – came from Kensington, but most of them were

for the formal flower-garden which was made for Sarah on the east front. This was originally enclosed, to Sarah's annoyance, by Vanbrugh's 'out-boundary wall', a high barrier running south from the orangery and, as she protested, blocking the view from the bow-window room. The wall was soon demolished, but its central feature, the colossal piers, which were carved by Gibbons with 'frost work' and bulrushes and topped with urns brimming with stone flowers, now form part of the Hensington Gate.

Marlborough showed from the first a strong personal interest in the making of Blenheim gardens. The story goes that Henry Wise, being 'pitch'd on' by the Duke to plant his grounds, was cautioned that his master (then only fifty-five) might not have long to enjoy them. It was up to Wise to work some kind of miracle that would produce plantations of full-grown trees ready-made. No doubt Marlborough had heard about the mature lime trees which Wise had transplanted at Hampton Court. He was equally successful at Blenheim, where the 'elms out the country' chosen for the two main avenues (east and north) with few exceptions took root and flourished.

In the same way that Vanbrugh delegated to Hawksmoor in the palace, he relied on Wise for helping to change the landscape in the neglected park. Wise, we know, was a gardener in a thousand; no job was too big for him. He undertook, to start with, the digging of the palace foundations through stiff clay to rock, and later was responsible for the causeway carrying the road over the Grand Bridge.

'The Garden wall was set agoing', Vanbrugh told the Duke, 'the Same day with the House; and I hope will be done against your Grace's return . . . The Kitchen garden Walls will likewise be so advanc'd that all the Plantations may be made.' The gardens were planned in two main parts: the Great Parterre (with its Woodwork) and the Walled Kitchen Garden which, though concealed half a mile from the palace, was in form and produce to be the finest of its kind. Fashion ruled that everything within sight of the house should be formal and symmetrical; and although Blenheim's garden was less so than some, it was yet extreme enough to be decried as stiff and unnatural by some critics. No wonder then that when 'Capability' Brown's 'desolating hand' descended on Blenheim the Great Parterre was swept away.

THE ITALIAN GARDEN

The Italian Garden, on the site of the 1st Duchess's garden, took its present form at the beginning of this century when it was re-created by the 9th Duke and Achille Duchêne. Its sheltered position, between the east wing and the south-facing orangery, is delightful enough. Originally it was to have been still more secluded, by Vanbrugh's high wall, but Sarah preferred to have a vista, and so it is that from her bow-window, now that of the private dining-room, there is no interruption to the view.

In these patterned beds with their dwarf box hedges, there is a pleasing reminder of the Great Parterre which once adjoined this garden on the south. It is an echo which recurs too in the Mermaid Fountain, made by the American sculptor Waldo Story, who lived in Rome and whose busts of the 9th Duke and Duchess can be seen in the north-west corridor of the palace.

When the 9th Duke succeeded to the title in 1892 he found here, as well as on the west front, a typical Victorian shrubbery, gloomy and meaningless. Using his knowledge of great gardens in France and Italy, he worked to give Blenheim the setting it deserved. First he replanted the Great Avenue with nearly 4,000 yards (3,700 metres) of elms, like opposing ranks at the Battle of Blenheim, leading northward from the Column of Victory to Akeman Street and the Ditchley Gate. After repaving the Great Court (grassed over by 'Capability' Brown), he called in

Duchêne to design for the east front
this formal garden which, in spite of its
name, might easily pass for the *jardin
d'honneur* of a French château.
Duchêne was a fervent admirer of the
gardens of André Le Nôtre. With its
crisp evergreen topiary, this garden is
pleasing at all seasons and never
more so than when the orange-trees
stand out in their tubs, when the
fountain is playing and the pink rose
called Caroline Testout scents the
south-east corner.

**The plan for the pedestal of
the sundial in the Italian Garden,
possibly by Hawksmoor**

**The mermaid fountain in
the Italian Garden**

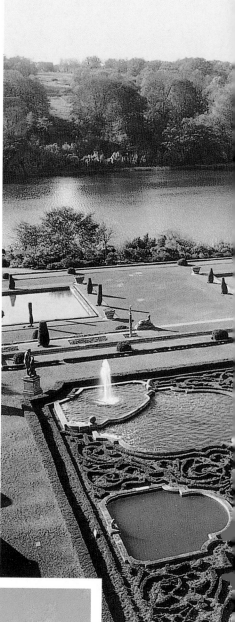

THE WATER TERRACES

By 1925 the 9th Duke had restored the formal setting of the palace on the north and east, and turned his attention to the west, where there was another confused jumble of shrubs. The transformation he planned with Duchêne was ambitious, costly and time-consuming. Duke and architect did not always see eye to eye. Duchêne was soon told to work less in the spirit of Le Nôtre than of Bernini, whose fountain was to have the place of honour on the second terrace; and when later Duchêne pleaded for fountains and running water, he was firmly put in his place. 'Limpidity of water', he was reminded, 'is pleasing and possesses a romance. You have got this effect in the basins and in the large area of water contained by the Lake. Be careful not to destroy this major emotion which Nature has granted to you for the sake of what may possibly be a vulgar display of waterworks which can be seen at any exhibition or public park. Turn all these matters over in your mind', the Duke added, 'when you are at rest in the evening, for it is only by thought, constant thought and mature reflection that artists have left their great works for the enjoyment of posterity.'

These terraces are reminiscent, on a smaller scale, of the *Parterre d'Eau* at Versailles. As well as the Bernini and

its answering obelisk, they have other unusual aspects, such as the lead sphinxes, their features those of the 9th Duke's second Duchess, and the caryatids, carved *in situ* by Visseau, which support the first terrace and are flanked by tiers of shells.

During five years of planning and building, an immense amount of thought and work went into the making of these terraces, yet some things happened by chance. A young gardener, who had been working on the Duchess's Rock Garden, happened to stroll by as Visseau was beginning to

Left: **The Bernini river-gods' fountain on the second Water Terrace (a *modello* for the river-gods' fountain in Rome's Piazza Navona)**

carve the caryatids, was stopped and asked if he would like to be immortalised. He thought he would. And so it is that the model for the head and torso of the northernmost caryatid was a local craftsman, Bert Timms of Hanborough.

When at last, in 1930, the terraces were finished, the Duke was magnanimous enough to congratulate Duchêne and to acknowledge his genius in an inscription on the south wall of the chapel.

In 1932, two years before the 9th Duke's death, Sir Sacheverell Sitwell urged him to re-create the parterre on the south lawn, even if it only meant 'some sort of patterning that would avoid all the expense of incessant cutting and trimming'. The Duke smiled and shrugged. He would have liked to do it but knew it was impossible.

THE ARBORETUM

From the lower Water Terrace a southward drive slopes up past cedars and winds on past the Temple of Diana, built for the 4th Duke by Sir William Chambers. This unpretentious temple stands on a high point, commanding a view over the lake to the woods. It was here, during the summer of 1908, that Mr Winston Churchill, as he then was, proposed to Miss Clementine Hozier, who was to become Baroness Churchill. In 1975 (European Architectural Heritage Year) the present Duke of Marlborough restored this temple and added two plaques, unveiled by Lady Churchill on 11th April of that year. 'There was a bench there then,' she remembered, 'and as I sat there with Winston I watched a beetle slowly moving across the floor. "If that beetle reaches that crack," I said to myself, "and Winston hasn't proposed, then he isn't going to." But he did propose!'

As the drive, called the Sheep Walk, continues, four incense cedars, each over 50 feet (15 metres) high, can be seen towering above the yew and prunus. This area of the gardens also contains specimens of other interesting and rare trees and shrubs, and is particularly attractive in spring, when the blossom is out and the grassy banks are covered in daffodils and bluebells.

The delightful Rose Garden, on the right, is contained within a circular walk, arched over by slender hoops supporting climbing roses of a delicate pink. The central feature, a pool with a statue, is surrounded by symmetrical beds of roses in shades of red, pink and white. The simple Temple of Flora also stands on the right, and just beyond it a group of beeches divides the path. The left fork dips towards giant cedars before bending right to reach the Grand Cascade.

Clockwise from right: **Oaks on the South Lawn; incense cedars, with cedar deodar in the foreground; the Temple of Flora; copper beech and Irish yews; a sunken path leads to the cascade; three Japanese trees:** *Prunus* **'Kanzan', hybrid crab apple** *Malus floribunda* **and maple** *Acer palmatum* **'Atropurpureum'; Judas tree; cedars of Lebanon**
Below: **The Rose Garden**

THE GRAND CASCADE

The Grand Cascade, designed by 'Capability' Brown in the 1760s, lets the Glyme fall from the lake to become a slow river, winding south-westwards, under Sir William Chambers' New Bridge until, with a further fall in the area known as the Lince, it joins the Evenlode, a tributary of the Thames. England has higher falls than the Grand Cascade but few more picturesque or, in spate, more boisterous. 'When the full stream devolves from the rocky barrier', wrote a visitor in 1790, 'and bounds from one point to another in foamy pride with deafening roar, nothing can be more grateful to a contemplative mind than such a scene and such a situation.' It was the 4th Duke's aim to remind his guests of the savage scenes painted by Salvator Rosa. While they threaded their way along the steep bank above the fall and with the roar of it in their ears, they suddenly found the path blocked by an enormous boulder. Filled with dismay, the guests watched as their host stepped forward to touch a hidden spring; whereupon the boulder swung back and admitted them to 'a spot in the highest style of picturesque beauty', where the Bernini Fountain (now on the Water Terraces) had been set up by Sir William Chambers.

When the 5th Duke succeeded, in 1817, he set himself to make 'the finest botanical and flower garden in England', and most of it was made just here, below and about the cascade. In this he was encouraged by his Duchess, whose exquisite paintings of flowers are in the Long Library; and still more by the new varieties of plants then arriving in Britain from abroad. The Duke bought and planned on a ducal scale. Down by the river he made the New Holland or Botany Bay Garden, the Chinese Garden and the Dahlia Garden, 'all surrounded with borders of seedling oaks, kept constantly cut'; whilst high up among trees and mossy boulders stood the Swiss Cottage ('the residence of the watchman to the Private Gardens') and the Druid's Temple ('an altar formed by an immense tablet of rock'). At a little distance below the fall, where the Glyme had become tranquil, a small island was graced with a rustic shelter called the Shepherd's Cot. What with grottoes, fountains, bridges, a Sylvan Bower and a Trysting Tree, this Valley of Streams must have been the perfect place for a picnic. Some of the great trees – cedar and swamp-cypress – are still there, and so of course are the cascade and the Swiss Bridge before it. Above the falls, stepping-stones were added by the 10th Duke; but the Rock Garden created there by the 5th Duke as 'a bold and rugged background' has long since reverted to its natural state.

THE LAKE AND THE BRIDGE

When in the winter of 1704–5 Marlborough and his architect, John Vanbrugh, surveyed Queen Anne's gift of Woodstock Park and chose the site for the palace, they realised that in direct line with its main (north-western) approach lay an awkward valley, wide, deep and precipitous, through which trickled the Glyme stream and its tributaries, forming a marsh. To cross this marsh there were two raised causeways with small bridges, used as shortcuts to Woodstock and Oxford; and, formerly, as two ways for pedestrians to approach Woodstock Manor.

Vanbrugh saw this marsh as ornamental water crossed by the finest bridge in Europe. Marlborough, more cautious, consulted Wren, who prescribed a far less pretentious and less costly bridge and, for the steep palace approach, a sweeping circular drive. His plan, 'stuck full of pins' as Vanbrugh described it, was not adopted. Vanbrugh's persuasiveness, which was considerable, won the day.

If Wren had had his way, a bridge only 15 feet (4.6 metres) high would have carried the grand approach over the Glyme; whereas the arcade on the top of Vanbrugh's, though never completed, was planned to have soared to 80 feet (24 metres).

When in 1708 the bridge was founded, there were still gargantuan problems, not the least of them how to link it with the sides of the valley. Marlborough had more than once to be reassured by Queen Anne's gardener, Henry Wise, and by Vanbrugh that they would find enough earth to fill the chasm, even though it meant levelling the hill on which the ruins of Woodstock Manor stood and using some of that masonry as rubble filling for the bridge.

Bartholomew Peisley, the mason who built the bridge, under Vanbrugh's direction, was 'very proud and overjoyed' when in 1710 the main arch,

From the falls the path continues beside the lake and back towards the palace. The boathouse was built for the 8th Duke and his second (American) Duchess in 1888. Across its lakeside gable runs the inscription, 'So may thy craft glide gently on as years roll down the stream.' For the more energetic, rowing-boats may be hired.

101 feet (almost 31 metres) wide, was keyed, 'it being a great and nice piece of work'.

Everything about the bridge is extraordinary and much of it is puzzling. No ground plan has survived. All we have is an elevation showing the proposed superstructure in the manner of a viaduct or of the Pont du Garde. Sarah 1st Duchess of Marlborough vetoed the arcade. 'I made Mr. Vanbrugh my enemy', she wrote, 'by the constant disputes I had with him to prevent his extravagance.' The immensity of the Grand Bridge and its cost was one of the main subjects of their dispute. The Duchess scathingly told a friend that she had counted thirty-three rooms in it, that there was a house at each corner and that what made it so much prettier than London Bridge was that you might 'set in six rooms and look out at window' while the coaches rumbled over your head. Vanbrugh in its defence went so far as to assure her that if, when it was finished, she found a house inside it she would go and live in it. Nothing was more unlikely; and indeed there is no

evidence that it was ever lived in, though some rooms have fireplaces and chimneys, and one large windowless chamber has been plastered and fitted with an elliptical arch as though for a theatre. Old guidebooks describe the bridge as a cool retreat in summer, and no doubt many a picnic was enjoyed in the sunnier rooms. Unfortunately it is no longer safe to enter now.

Soon after Marlborough's death, in 1722, his widow called in Colonel John Armstrong, who had been his chief engineer, to replan the water-works in the park. The River Glyme, flowing under the Grand Bridge, was channelled into canals that beneath the middle arch leapt a cascade before broadening into a formal pool on the western side.

The northernmost arch of the bridge was used to house Aldersea's engine, a huge paddle-wheel affair,

The Grand Bridge with arcaded superstructure and drumhead finials as planned by Vanbrugh (*above*) **was never completed;** (*below*) **the Grand Bridge today**

which pumped spring water from Rosamond's Well to the East Gate cistern. This stood on the leads, where the flag now flies, and provided the eastern half of the palace with water. As a water-supply it worked well but, as scenery, the canals looked inadequate and called forth such quips as Pope's:

'The minnows, as under this vast arch they pass, murmur, "How like whales we look, thanks to your Grace!"'

To judge from old engravings, the canal and pool Sarah favoured looked very bleak – the pool itself was designed with a compass and was like a huge version of the Versailles fountain-basins. But formality was the fashion, and for those who admired it the results at Blenheim brought praise. Sarah herself was delighted. 'The canal and basin', she told her suitor, the Duke of Somerset, in 1723, 'look very fine. There is to be a lake and a cascade on the side of the Bridge next Woodstock . . . Sir John [Vanbrugh] never thought of this cascade,' she complacently adds, 'which will be the finest & largest that ever was made . . . The fine green meadow

between the house & the wood is to remain as it is, and I believe your Grace will think in that, Nature cannot be mended, tho' Sir John formerly set his heart upon turning that into a lake, as I will do it on the other side, and I will have swans & all such sort of things . . .'

When Sarah died in 1744, Blenheim waited twenty years before reflecting the change of fashion from formality to naturalism in its own magnificent lake. Then, with one master-stroke, 'Capability' Brown was able to change the landscape. After building a dam and cascade near Bladon, he sliced through the causeways once leading from Woodstock Manor across the marsh towards Woodstock and Oxford, leaving a small strip now known as Queen Elizabeth's Island. Thus he let the Glyme run through the bridge, engulfing the ground floor, and spread out into lakes on either side of it. Another mile downstream Brown made minor cascades of great beauty at the point where the Glyme falls into the Evenlode. This then joins the Thames, which he boasted would never forgive him.

'If these two lakes had been designed as one vast expanse of water,' comments Brown's biographer, Dorothy Stroud, 'the effect would have been tedious. As it is they are both united yet divided by Vanbrugh's bridge, from which the two parts spread out like the loops of a nicely tied bow.'

Above: **A view of the palace across the lake with Queen Elizabeth's Island**
Below: **The canal-and-pool scheme devised by Marlborough's widow and his chief engineer**

True, the cascade Sarah had been so proud of is now under water; but Brown's Grand Cascade still tumbles into the lake at its western end.

At the Grand Bridge the northern arch had been cleared of its engine before the ground-floor rooms were flooded. This last event caused much anxiety. Could the bridge withstand it? It could and did. But the visible height of the bridge is now a great deal less than Vanbrugh intended. Its base is submerged, and the arcaded superstructure with which Vanbrugh planned to crown it has never been built.

'The lake at Blenheim', wrote Sir Sacheverell Sitwell, 'is the one great argument of the landscape gardener. There is nothing finer in Europe.'

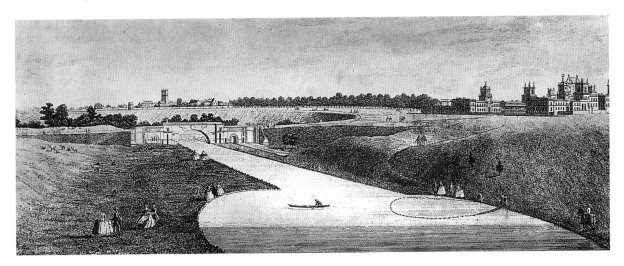

ROSAMOND'S WELL

Rosamond's Well, once known as Everswell, is the oldest thing at Blenheim and by association the most romantic: the spring that has never dried up, the same that was known to Henry II's lover, Rosamond Clifford. In the legend of Fair Rosamond, discovered in her bower and stabbed or poisoned by a jealous queen, truth and fiction seem as intricately entangled as were the winding paths of the labyrinth the King is said to have devised for her. Whatever that labyrinth was, very few were allowed to see it. Now, however, thanks to recent research, we know much more of the buildings that stood there and of their origin. There were at first three pools, the largest surrounded by a cloister and neighboured by a group of buildings called 'Rosamond' – a sort of Trianon, later to be used as a retreat where royalty could escape from the formality of the court at Woodstock Manor. In H.M. Colvin's view, 'One of the most agreeable features of Everswell must have been the Queen's garden, which was laid out round one of the pools.' He suggests that the idea of a house with water running through it may have come from Sicily, with which the court of Henry II had close connections; or it may have been at least partly inspired by the twelfth-century romance of Tristan and Isolde, a version of which is believed to have been written for Henry II. In that legend the lovers are supposed to have met in an orchard near the royal castle in which Isolde lived. 'This orchard was surrounded by a strong palisade and at one end of it there was a spring from which water first filled a marble pool and then continued in a narrow channel which ran through Isolde's apartment in such a way that Tristan was able to communicate with her by dropping twigs into the stream . . . Everswell, in fact,' concludes Colvin, 'provided the complete *mise-en-scène* of the poetic episode.' (R.A. Brown, H.M. Colvin and A.J. Taylor, *The History of the King's Works, II, The Middle Ages,* HMSO, London, pp. 1010-17.)

Legends die hard and of the many persisting here one at least insists on the magic properties of Rosamond's spring water. The 9th Duke had it piped the length of the lake and then pumped up to his Water Terraces and to his kitchens. When the water was analysed, nothing miraculous was found, but, compared with present-day tap-water, the taste is delicious.

The well also provided the inspiration for establishing a Bottling

Below: **An unexecuted plan for a bathing-house at Rosamond's Well, about 1770**

Plant in the Palace grounds. It is from here that the famous Blenheim Natural Mineral Water now comes – a prestigious mineral water which can be found in some of the finest hotels and restaurants in the country.

THE TRIUMPHAL ARCH

The Triumphal Arch, raised in Marlborough's honour by his widow in 1723, is now used as the chief entrance from Woodstock. Its architect was Nicholas Hawksmoor, who had collaborated with Vanbrugh in the building of the palace; his pattern for this gateway being a Roman ruin, possibly the Arch of Titus. 'I fear it will be thought too narrow for the height,' wrote Sarah, when it was almost finished, 'though when Lord Burlington saw it he found no fault with that.' Certainly it is very narrow indeed. Yet the effect on the visitor who for the first time passes through it, to have the whole vast view suddenly burst on him, is tremendous. 'It is not', wrote Boydell, 'a transition from nothing to something but from nothing to everything.'

On the Woodstock side the arch carries a Latin inscription, and on the Blenheim side is the translation:

This gate was built the year after the death of the most illustrious John, Duke of Marlborough, by order of Sarah his most beloved wife, to whom he left the sole direction of the many things that remained unfinished of this fabric. The services of this great man to his country the pillar will tell you which the Duchess has erected for a lasting monument of his glory and her affection to him. MDCCXXIII.

THE COLUMN OF VICTORY

The Column of Victory, which was begun five years after Marlborough's death, was finished in 1730 and cost about £3,000. The height of this Doric column, surmounted by eagles, is 134 feet (40 metres), including the lead statue of the Duke, by Robert Pit, an otherwise unknown craftsman. The statue holds aloft a winged Victory 'as an ordinary man might hold a bird'.

Before the final design was adopted, a great many proposals were made, both as to the shape of the monument and its position. For some years the plan had been to have an obelisk, standing halfway along the Great Avenue, and Nicholas Hawksmoor prepared designs. This obelisk would probably have had a stairway so that visitors might appreciate the pattern of the elms. An alternative site was considered to mark the position of Woodstock Manor and to 'give an opportunity of mentioning that King [Henry II] whose Scenes of Love Sir John [Vanbrugh] was so much pleas'd with'. But that suggestion did not appeal to the Duchess. 'If there were obelisks to bee made of what all our Kings have don of that sort,' she wrote over it, 'the countrey would bee Stuffed with very odd things.' She finally chose the present site, at the entrance to the Great Avenue and, having looked over a number of measured drawings by Hawksmoor and others, called in Lord Herbert and his assistant Roger Morris, architect of the Palladian Bridge at Wilton and of the stables at Althorp, to 'conduct' its completion.

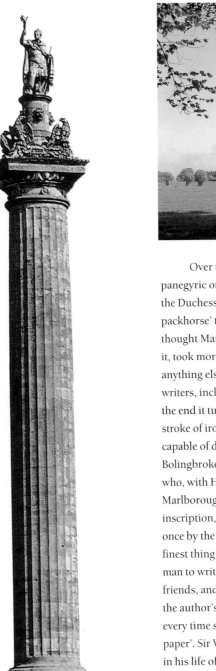

Over the inscription (the panegyric on the side facing the palace) the Duchess, 'labouring like a packhorse' to finish Blenheim as she thought Marlborough would have liked it, took more trouble than with anything else, trying many different writers, including Alexander Pope. In the end it turned out, by an unlikely stroke of irony, that the only man capable of doing it justice was Lord Bolingbroke (Henry St John), the man who, with Harley, had plotted the Marlboroughs' downfall. His inscription, however, was recognised at once by the shrewd Duchess as 'the finest thing that was possible for any man to write'. She sent copies to her friends, and while carefully concealing the author's identity, admitted that every time she read it she 'wet the paper'. Sir Winston Churchill observes in his life of Marlborough, 'The inscription is a masterpiece of compact and majestic statement. In fact, it would serve as a history in itself, were all other records lost.'

THE LODGES

The grounds of Blenheim contain a number of lodges and cottages, and a farm, none of which is open to the public. High Lodge is the oldest of the lodges, and its situation due west of the palace, on the far side of the lake, is the highest. When John Wilmot, Earl of Rochester and Ranger of Woodstock Park for Charles II, died there in 1680, it was a farmhouse with hipped roof and gables. Vanbrugh added to the building in about 1710 to make it more comfortable for Marlborough and his Duchess, who liked to stay there while the palace was being built. History is then silent about the lodge until the close of the eighteenth century, when Dr W.F. Mavor in a guidebook, *New Description of Blenheim*, refers to its 'antique battlements', which must in fact have been added by the 4th Duke, probably with the help of 'Capability' Brown, who had been transforming barns at Park Farm, north-west of the Column of Victory, to a gothic design. Whoever adapted High Lodge turned it into a toy castle and so it looks today, reflected in its reservoir or seen in the distance among venerable oaks.

In the 9th Duke's day, when the Prince and Princess of Wales attended his shooting-party, High Lodge made a romantic background for a group photograph.

Boydell's engraving of High Lodge in 1752

'Methinks if such good fortune ever befell a bookish man,' wrote the American author Nathaniel Hawthorne, 'I should choose this lodge for my own residence, with the topmost room of the tower for a study and all the seclusion of cultivated wilderness beneath to ramble in.'

Of the other lodges that Marlborough knew, the largest was North Lodge, near Ditchley Gate. This he intended for his old friend Brigadier-General Cadogan, who had served with him in his campaigns; but as Sarah observed in 1713, 'to be sure he will never make use of it'. Instead it was allotted to a gamekeeper. Springlock Lodge, named after the 'magic' boulder above the Grand Cascade, is of later date, as are Water Meadow Lodge, near Hanborough Lodge, the Lince Lodge,

and the China Corner, built to house the 4th Duke's collection of china. Sarah talked of rebuilding Bladon Lodge; and she may also have known the Fishery Cottage near Seven Arches where the Glyme enters the park from Old Woodstock and flows into the lake. The story goes that at the Hensington Gate, due east of the palace, where the Oxford road reaches Woodstock, the 1st Duchess was defied by a gardener who owned a small plot there and refused to sell it. 'No, Sarah,' he is supposed to have said, 'go round the other way.' Though this takes some believing, no better explanation is known for the oblique approach through the Triumphal Arch (effective, but at that date unorthodox), nor for the making of Hensington Gate, with the colossal piers designed for Sarah's flower garden, long after her death in 1744.

Left: **High Lodge as background to the royal shooting-party of 1896. The group includes the Prince and Princess of Wales (later King Edward VII and Queen Alexandra) and the 9th Duke and Duchess of Marlborough with, on her right, Sir Winston Churchill's mother, Lady Randolph Churchill (front row, second from left)**

WOODSTOCK MANOR

On a green promontory near the
northern end of the bridge and on its
eastern side, there stands a very large
sycamore, overhanging the water.
This tree, and another like it, were
planted over two and three-quarter
centuries ago to commemorate
Woodstock Manor, the royal hunting-
box which Sarah found in ruins and,
in 1709, directed to be pulled down.
More recently a stone memorial has
been placed on the site. The plinth of
this was designed by Sir William
Chambers.

Legend has helped to obscure the
manor's beginnings. Henry I, we know,
walled the park for his deer and
menagerie; but what exactly were the
bower and labyrinth Henry II built
there for Rosamond Clifford? Only her
never-failing spring (with the square
'well' where she is said to have bathed)
remains. Henry's hunting lodge, a
separate but unambitious building, was
rebuilt and added to by succeeding
sovereigns until, by the time Elizabeth I
came to be imprisoned there in 1554-5
for her alleged part in the Wyatt plot, it
had become a quite impressive range of
halls, chapels, courts and offices. It
even had a garden and a tennis-court;
though the main exercise and enter-
tainment was hunting the deer through
Wychwood Forest. The manor's long
history is one of obstinate resilience;
and in spite of the harsh battering it
had suffered from Cromwell's soldiers,
it was still habitable, or at least so
Vanbrugh considered, when he first
explored it in 1705.

To Vanbrugh, a romantic born
before his time, the appeal of the ruined
manor was immediate. He would have
preserved it for the legend of Fair
Rosamond alone, but there were other
advantages. It was handy for Blenheim
works, and he installed a forge there.
Most important, in the general
panorama and especially in the

Woodstock Manor

northern view from the palace it would
make 'One of the Most Agreeable
Objects that the best of Landskip
Painters could invent'. He directed
palace workmen to make it a 'little
decent' and to keep the 'habitable part'
from tumbling down. Which was well
enough. But in 1713, while the
Marlboroughs were abroad, he went
further, moving in his 'household stuff'.
He continued to live in the manor, on
and off, for three years; a piece of
impudence which irrevocably widened
the rift between himself and the
Duchess. Of course in the end he had to
move and indeed to leave Blenheim
altogether; but parts of Woodstock
Manor were still standing when
Marlborough died in 1722. Much of the
old house was used, ironically enough,
as rubble filling for Vanbrugh's
Grand Bridge.

THE PARK

The dry-stone wall of Woodstock Park, said to have been the first park wall built in England, and in poor repair when the Marlboroughs took over in 1705, was not rebuilt until after the 1st Duke's death; nor was it finished until 1729. The masons were William Townsend of Oxford and Bartholomew Peisley junior, son of the master-mason who built the Grand Bridge. With their estimate (£1,196 per mile) they sent the Duchess a plan showing how the coping was designed to 'carry off wet' and shed the rain. The total length of the wall was between 8 and 9 miles (about 13 kilometres); the wall itself 2 feet (61 centimetres) thick and 8 feet (2.4 metres) high, allowing 1 foot (30 centimetres) for foundation. Considering all things, it has lasted well. Even so it calls for constant maintenance, if only to make good the breaches caused by the falling of trees or of rotten boughs. This is skilled work, and few masons can now be found to do it.

The 9th Duke of Marlborough was responsible for planting no fewer than 465,000 trees in and about Blenheim Park between 1893 and 1919. 'The planting of oaks in the High Park', he wrote in 1898, 'should be continued for another 25 years, and then the Park will be stocked for 500 years to come.' Two years before that he had begun to replant the Northern Avenue with elms (where the Column of Victory stands), 'believing that in the year 2000 it will form a remarkable feature in the Park, extending as it does for nearly two miles; and any man who cuts these trees down', he added, 'for the purpose of selling the timber is a scoundrel and deserves the worst fate that can befall him.'

Between Bladon Gate and New Bridge he planted three lakeside clumps, 'hoping for the following effect: that a person passing the Bridge will first see a mass of copper beech, followed by another mass of grey glaucous cedars, and again beyond, yet another mass of copper beech. I believe that the combination of the two colours, the copper and the grey, ought to be most effective and picturesque' – a prediction, as we see today, most happily fulfilled.

'The Old Park with its oaks and bracken', the Duke noted in 1900, 'was meant to remain as an example to all time of the imposing effect of a medieval forest. In a similar way the Column of Victory and Low Park, where the elms were planted in avenues, were meant to convey to the observer the idea and style of the age of Queen Anne, the period when the house was built. It has been my aim in all the planting I have given orders to be carried out to preserve those peculiarities and characteristics of Blenheim Park.'

More recently Blenheim Park has been badly hit by freak storms, which brought down many of the trees planted in the times of the 1st and 4th Dukes; and also by Dutch elm disease which, in spite of every precaution, destroyed the two main avenues of elms, on the north and on the east.

However, the present Duke has already had both these avenues replanted – the Northern Avenue with limes and the Eastern Avenue, renamed the Jubilee Avenue, with alternate lime and plane trees. The first of the limes on the south side of Jubilee Avenue was planted by His Royal Highness the Prince of Wales on 19th December 1976. In addition, the Duke has overseen the completion of the initial phase of the first twenty-five years of the phased park restoration plan which is cyclic and covers the next two centuries. He has also had many thousands of parkland and commercial trees planted.

THE PRIVATE GARDEN

East and south of the Italian Garden lie areas which are not open to visitors: the Duke's croquet-lawn and private garden (begun in 1954), with between them one of the four sundials made for the 1st Duke by John Rowley, the mathematician commissioned by Wren for the great dial at St Paul's. The design for the pedestal survives. The dial itself has a pin pierced with the 1st Duke's arms and gives a table 'which by the first of March sheweth the day of the month forever'.

To the south, the drive bordering the Duke's garden (with, beyond it, the Temple of Health), leads through a cedar grove to the Roundabout or Exedra. This circular arrangement of clipped yew and box, in alternating segments, is so planned as to provide vistas in twelve directions. The Exedra was planted in the nineteenth century, and the central group of gambolling children is derived from sculpture in the groves of Versailles. The trees in this part of the grounds are notable: cedar, oak, hornbeam, and a romantic group of four lombardy poplars, standing between the Exedra and the pond.

THE WALLED KITCHEN GARDEN

This kitchen garden of 8 acres (3.2 hectares), enclosed within brick walls 14 feet (4 metres) high, with Taynton stone dressings, was planned by Vanbrugh and Wise to echo the martial theme of the military garden north-west of it; and so it too has 100-foot (30-metre) bastions, smaller than those designed for the State Garden, to which it was set at an angle to ensure due-south-facing walls.

The building of these walls, begun in 1705, was undertaken by Thomas Churchill and Richard Stacey, the master-bricklayers who built Queen Anne's orangery at Kensington Palace. By coincidence, a namesake of the gardener's, one Henry Wise of Hanborough, contracted to supply 500,000 'good, well-burnt, statutable bricks' at eighteen shillings (90p) a thousand.

Marlborough's intense interest in this part of the work is reflected in his letters to his Duchess. 'If you have the same weather', he wrote from the heat of his camp at Meldert in June 1707, 'it must make all sorts of fruit very good; and as this is the third year of the trees at Woodstock, if possible I should wish that you might . . . taste the fruit of every tree, so that what is not good might be changed. On this matter you must advise with Mr. Wise, as also what plan may be proper for the ice-house, for that should be built this summer . . .'

After visiting the nursery Henry Wise ran at Brompton Park in Kensington with his partner George London, the diarist John Evelyn noted: 'They have a very brave and noble assembly of the flowering and other trees, and of perennial and variegated evergreens and shrubs, hardy and fittest for our climate; and understand what best to plant the humble boscage, wilderness or taller groves with . . . and all within one enclosure.'

The ice-house, near the park's south-eastern boundary, had some

years ago to be closed and abandoned; but the kitchen garden walls are still in excellent shape, though pitted with holes where generations of gardeners have nailed their espaliers.

In the summer of 1716 Vanbrugh wrote to Marlborough: 'The Kitchen Garden, now the trees are in full vigour and full of fruit, is really an astonishing sight. All I ever saw in England or abroad of the kind are trifles to it.' Wise recommended twenty-eight varieties of peach and seventy-two of pear; and in fact, as time went on, every delectable kind of peach and nectarine, plum and pear was grown there. Figs ripened on the bastions, while mulberries and quinces, apples and cherries grew in the old orchard beyond the south wall.

On the central line of the Walled Garden round pools of water made decorative reservoirs; while heading a niche in the northern wall hangs the bell which once summoned a regiment of gardeners or signalled their time for going home. The garden itself, within its original walls, has been adapted to make it workable in modern conditions. Vanbrugh's brick and stone frame is still there as, in the western wall, is the Palladian Gateway, added in the 4th Duke's time by Sir William Chambers. Muscats still grow in the vinery; other luxuries, such as the orchids and car-nations grown for the 9th Duke, have had to go. A variety of shrubs has been planted. The Marlborough Maze, planted in 1988 within the Walled Garden, was opened to the public in 1991.

BLENHEIM PARK RAILWAY

This narrow-gauge railway acts as a link between the palace car park and the Pleasure Gardens. The railway operates daily throughout the season (from mid-March to the end of October) at half-hourly intervals. The diesel locomotive, *Sir Winston Churchill*, pulls three canopied carriages and can reach a speed of 12 mph.

THE PLEASURE GARDENS

The Pleasure Gardens complex is formed around the Walled Garden, the original kitchen garden of the palace, which now contains the Marlborough Maze. Although it continues to provide fresh fruit, including prize-winning grapes, and vegetables for the palace, as well as hot-house flowers and shrubs, the whole area now leans more to the enjoyment of Blenheim's visitors. At the entrance is the purpose-built garden cafeteria of a pleasing, modern design where visitors can refresh themselves and look out over the peaceful parkland. Adjacent is the herb garden, with trellis walks, pergolas and separate beds of lavender and herbs, walled with mellow brick topped with slate to reflect the material used in the Victorian buildings adjoining. Within the maze area is a model of a Woodstock street, putting greens, as well as giant chess and draughts. Indeed, together with the Butterfly House, and combined with a visit to the palace and park, there is something for all the family – a complete day out.

THE BUTTERFLY HOUSE

In the Butterfly House exotic tropical butterflies can be seen in free flight. The special hatchery contains the pupae of many of the species, so a large number of the plants grown in the main flight section are nectar plants to provide food for the adult butterflies. This makes the main house a virtually natural habitat for these beautiful creatures. It is possible to study the full life-cycle.

Butterflies to be seen at Blenheim will vary from month to month; over one hundred tropical species are bred, over the season. Most butterflies live for a matter of weeks, so there is often a succession of broods through the summer from some of the species.

More exotic butterflies include the Monarch, from North America, which migrates hundreds of miles each summer and autumn, the Owl butter-flies of Central and South America,

THE FUTURE OF BLENHEIM

The future of Blenheim must to a large degree depend on its visitors. Without their support and goodwill, it would be impossible to meet the rising costs of maintenance and restoration, conservation and tree-planting. Major capital projects, such as dredging the lake and rewiring the palace, are very real and serious problems, for which additional funds must be found. Every penny given by visitors goes towards these ever-increasing costs and additional forms of fund-raising are constantly being considered.

In 1986, the Duke and family trustees donated £1.5 million towards the creation of the Blenheim Foundation, which aims to raise money to secure the upkeep of the palace in perpetuity. In the words of the present Duke, 'Whilst Blenheim was given to my ancestor and is still owned by my family, my role today is virtually that of a trustee and custodian of Blenheim – not only for Britain, but for all those in every part of the world who cherish the historical and artistic tradition that Blenheim represents.'

In 1988 Blenheim Palace was named as one of only four special sites in the United Kingdom for inclusion in the World Heritage List; a distinction very much in keeping with its traditions and values.

which use the owl markings on the underside of their wings as a defence, and the Heliconius butterflies, which are also natives of Central and South America. These can live for several months, feeding on pollen, which gives more sustenance than nectar.

In a special enclosure in the hatching-area can usually be seen a selection of insects, including stick insects, praying mantis, beetles and giant millipedes.

Since butterflies and insects are natural creatures there is inevitably variation over time in what might be seen.

THE MARLBOROUGH MAZE

The Marlborough Maze is the world's largest symbolic hedge maze, designed to reflect the history and architectural magnificence of the palace. The lines of hedges portray the splendour of the victory at Blenheim in symbolic form. Their shapes, inspired by the trophies carved by Grinling Gibbons for the east and west colonnades, include trumpets, banners and cannonballs, as well as giant cannon. The maze covers an area of just over an acre (0.4 hectare) and has two brick and stone pavilions and two high wooden bridges which provide perfect vantage points.

THE DUKES OF MARLBOROUGH

JOHN: FIRST DUKE

HENRIETTA: SECOND DUCHESS

CHARLES: THIRD DUKE

GEORGE: FOURTH DUKE

GEORGE: FIFTH DUKE

GEORGE: SIXTH DUKE

JOHN: SEVENTH DUKE

GEORGE: EIGHTH DUKE

CHARLES: NINTH DUKE

ALBERT: TENTH DUKE

JOHN: ELEVENTH DUKE

THE MARLBOROUGH (SPENCER-CHURCHILL) LINE OF DESCENT

Sir Winston Churchill = ELIZABETH DRAKE
b. 1620 — of Ashe, Devon

♛ **John**
b. 1650, cr. Duke of Marlborough* and K.G. 1702 cr. Prince of the Holy Roman Empire 1705. *d.* 16 June, 1722
= SARAH
dr. of Richard Jennings of St Albans *b.* 1660. *m.* 1678. *d.* 18 Oct., 1744

* Duke of Marlborough: a title which John Churchill is believed to have taken in consequence of a connection on his mother's side, with the family of Ley, earls of Marlborough, extinct ten years previously.

JOHN
Marquess of Blandford
b. 1686. *d.* 1703

♛ **Henrietta**
b. 1681. Suc. as Duchess of Marlb. 1722, s.p.m. *d.* 1733
= FRANCIS
2nd Earl of Godolphin

ANNE
b. 1684 *d.* 1716
= CHARLES SPENCER
K.G., 3rd Earl of Sunderland

ELIZABETH
b. 1687 *d.* 1714
= SCROOP
1st Duke of Bridgewater

MARY
b. 1689 *d.* 1751
= JOHN
2nd Duke of Montagu

ROBERT SPENCER
b. 1701. Suc. as Earl of Sund. 1722. *d.* unm. 1729

♛ **Charles Spencer**
b. 1706. Suc. as Earl of Sund. 1729 and as 3rd Duke of Marlb. 1733. K.G. *d.* 1758
= ELIZABETH
dr. of Earl Trevor

JOHN SPENCER
(Ancestor of the Earls Spencer)
= GEORGINA
dr. of Earl Granville

DIANA SPENCER
b. 1708. *d.* 1735
= JOHN
4th Duke of Bedford, K.G.

♛ **George Spencer**
4th Duke of Marlb. K.G., LL.D., F.R.S.
b. 1739. Suc. 1758. *d.* 1817
= CAROLINE
dr. of Duke of Bedford
b. 1743. *d.* 1811

†The 5th Duke was authorised in 1817 to 'take and use the name of Churchill, in addition to and after that of Spencer... in order to perpetuate in his Grace's family a surname to which his illustrious ancestor, John, first Duke of Marlborough, added such imperishable lustre'.

♛ **George Spencer-Churchill†**
5th Duke of Marlborough
b. 1766. Suc. 1817. *d.* 1840
= SUSAN
dr. of 7th Earl of Galloway
b. 1767. *d.* 1841

♛ **George Spencer-Churchill**
6th Duke of Marlborough
b. 1793. Suc. 1840. *d.* 1857
= (i) JANE, dr. of 8th Earl of Galloway. *d.* 1844
(ii) CHARLOTTE, dr. of Viscount Ashbrook. *d.* 1850
(iii) JANE, dr. of Hon. Edward Stewart. *d.* 1897

♛ **John Winston Spencer-Churchill**
7th Duke of Marlborough, K.G.
b. 1822. M.P. Suc. 1857 Gov. Gen. of Ireland 1876-80. *d.* 1883
= FRANCES
dr. of Marquess of Londonderry

♛ **George Charles Spencer-Churchill**
8th Duke of Marlborough
b. 1844. Suc. 1883. *d.* 1892
= (i) ALBERTHA
dr. of Duke of Abercorn
(ii) LILIAN
dr. of Cicero Price (U.S.A.)

RANDOLPH HENRY SPENCER-CHURCHILL
b. at Blenheim 1849
P.C., LL.D., etc. *d.* 1895
Buried at Bladon, Oxon
= JENNIE
dr. of Leonard Jerome (U.S.A.)
d. 1921

WINSTON LEONARD SPENCER-CHURCHILL
K.G., O.M., C.H., M.P., etc.
b. at Blenheim 30 Nov., 1874
d. 24 Jan., 1965. Buried at Bladon, Oxon
= CLEMENTINE D.B.E.
dr. of Sir Henry Montagu Hozier, K.C.B.
d. 12 Dec., 1977

♛ **Charles Richard John Spencer-Churchill**
9th Duke of Marlborough, K.G.
b. 1871. Suc. 1892. Sec. of State 1903-5 *d.* 1934
= (i) CONSUELO
dr. of William Vanderbilt (U.S.A.)
m. 1895 *d.* 1964
(ii) GLADYS
dr. of Edward Parker Deacon (U.S.A.)
m. 1921 *d.* 1977

♛ **John Albert Edward William Spencer-Churchill**
10th Duke of Marlborough, J.P., D.L.
b. 18 Sept., 1897. Suc. 1934 *d.* 1972
= (i) ALEXANDRA MARY CADOGAN
dr. of Viscount Chelsea
m. 1920
C.B.E., J.P.
Chief Comdt. A.T.S. 1938-40
d. 1961
(ii) LAURA
dr. of Hon. Guy Charteris
m. 1972

IVOR CHARLES SPENCER-CHURCHILL
b. 14 Oct., 1898
d. 1956

♛ **John George Vanderbilt Henry Spencer-Churchill**
11th Duke of Marlborough. J.P., D.L.
b. 13 April, 1926 Suc. 1972
= (i) SUSAN MARY
dr. of Michael Hornby
m. 1951
(ii) ATHINA MARY
dr. of Stavros G. Livanos
m. 1961
(iii) DAGMAR ROSITA
dr. of Count Carl Ludwig Douglas
m. 1972

CHARLES GEORGE WILLIAM COLIN SPENCER-CHURCHILL
b. 13 July, 1940
m. (i) 1965 Gillian Spreckels Fuller
(ii) 1970 Elizabeth Jane Wyndham

SARAH CONSUELO SPENCER-CHURCHILL *b.* 17 Dec., 1921
m. (i) 1943 Edwin F. Russell (U.S.N.R.)
(ii) 1966 Guy Burgos
(iii) 1967 Theodorous Roubanis

CAROLINE SPENCER-CHURCHILL
b. 12 Nov., 1923
m. 1946 Major Charles Hugo Waterhouse
d. 1992

ROSEMARY MILDRED SPENCER-CHURCHILL
b. 24 July, 1929
m. 1953 Charles Robert Muir

JOHN DAVID IVOR SPENCER-CHURCHILL
b. 1952. *d.* 1955

Charles James Spencer-Churchill
Marquis of Blandford
b. 24 Nov., 1955
= (i) REBECCA MARY FEW BROWN
m. 1990
(ii) EDLA GRIFFITHS
m. 2002

George John Godolphin Spencer-Churchill
Earl of Sunderland
b. 28 July, 1992

HENRIETTA MARY SPENCER-CHURCHILL
b. 1958
m. 1980
NATHAN GELBER

RICHARD SPENCER-CHURCHILL
b. 1973. *d.* 1973

EDWARD ALBERT CHARLES SPENCER-CHURCHILL
b. 1974

ALEXANDRA ELIZABETH MARY SPENCER-CHURCHILL
b. 1977

DAVID ABA GELBER
b. 1981

MAXIMILLIAN HENRY GELBER
b. 1985

1 **Visitors' entrance**
2 **Entrance to Palace**
3 **Entrance to – and only exit from – gardens**
4 **Cafeteria, restaurant and telephone**

5 **Water Terraces**
6 **To the Temple of Diana, Arboretum and Grand Cascade**
7 **To the Grand Bridge**
8 **To the narrow-gauge railway station**

G **Gift Shop**
O **The Orangery (Function Room)**

Visitors to Blenheim Palace and Park are requested to observe the notices, to park cars only where indicated, to keep to the drives and paths, to place litter in the containers provided and not to damage trees or plants. Dogs, on a leash, are allowed in the Park but not the Palace or Gardens unless they are guide dogs for the blind or hearing dogs for the deaf.

Further enquiries:
The Administrator, Blenheim Palace, Woodstock, Oxfordshire OX20 1PX.
Tel: 01993 811091
Fax: 01993 813527
Website: http://www.blenheimpalace.com
E-mail: administrator@blenheimpalace.com

BLENHEIM EDUCATION SERVICE

A full education service is available to all education establishments. Education visits may be made to the Palace, Park (including Nature Trail and Butterfly House), Forest, Gardens and the Marlborough Maze. The National Curriculum is particularly well provided for at all levels, whilst general and leisure interest visits are also well supported.

Blenheim has held the Sandford Award for an Outstanding Contribution to Heritage Education continuously since 1982.

Details from the Education Officer, Blenheim Palace, Woodstock, Oxfordshire OX20 1PX. Tel: 01993 811091 Fax: 01993 813527.

BLENHEIM VISITORS

The Palace is open daily, 10.30–17.30 (last admission 16.45) from mid-March to the end of October. The Park is open daily, 09.00–17.00 throughout the year. There are ample coach and car-parking areas close to the Palace entrance. Palace visitors may take a guided tour (five- to ten-minute intervals) or view the rooms independently. The tour of the Palace takes about an hour, but extra time should be allowed to see the Park and Gardens and visit the Pleasure Gardens. **Admission tickets to the Palace include the tour, Churchill Exhibition, Park, Gardens, Parking, Butterfly House and Train** (subject to availability, weather conditions, periodic maintenance or mechanical breakdown), and the use of Restaurants and Cafeterias. Entry to the Marlborough Maze, which includes the Adventure Play Area, is an optional extra.

Some 600 yards (550 metres) from the Palace, and accessible by train, on foot or by car, the Pleasure Gardens include the Marlborough Maze, Butterfly House, Garden Cafeteria, Adventure Play Area, putting greens, giant chess and draughts, and garden shop. The Pleasure Gardens, Marlborough Maze and Butterfly House are open daily, 10.00–18.00 mid-March to the end of October. The Garden Cafeteria is open all year.

THE BLENHEIM FOUNDATION

Information may be obtained from:
The Secretary, The Blenheim Foundation, Blenheim Palace, Woodstock, Oxfordshire OX20 1PX.

General information:
1 Occasionally it is necessary for furniture, paintings or other exhibits to be moved; or for room layouts to be altered. Therefore items referred to in the guidebook may not be on display, or may be displayed in other settings.
2 The right to close the Park or Palace without notice is reserved.
3 Extra facilities may be altered or withdrawn according to public demand.